is
anyone
out
there

is
anyone
out
there

D'LYNNE L AWRENCE

ARPress
ILLUMINATING IDEAS.
EMPOWERING VOICES

ARPress
45 Dan Road Suite 5
Canton MA 02021

Hotline: 1(888) 821-0229
Fax: 1(508) 545-7580

Ordering Information:
Quantity sales. Special discounts are available on quantity purchases by corporations, associations, and others. For details, contact the publisher at the address above.

Printed in the United States of America.

ISBN-13: Softcover   979-8-89356-713-7
          eBook   979-8-89356-714-4

Library of Congress Control Number: 2024904600

CONTENTS

MY LOVE

I met this man

Not just any man

He is perfect to a tee

And even with the luggage I bring

He still wants me to be me

When we first met

It was love from the start

Even the days seemed good

Everyone we met they fell in Love with him to

J   **just to be close to him you**

Could feel his love

E   **each day felt like a new beginning**

Just being with him

S   **sometime you would think he is**

Not of this world

U   **using his wisdom when he talks**

To smooth away yours hurt

S   **situation seem to change as**

Though he has a master key

His name is JESUS

And he is the only one for me

THE WIND

The wind always blows
East, West, North and South
Never really knowing which way to go

But to my surprised a dust cloud
Of wind form an eye and wink at me
As the wind went busily by

It made me laugh to see the wind wink
For it never knows which way to go

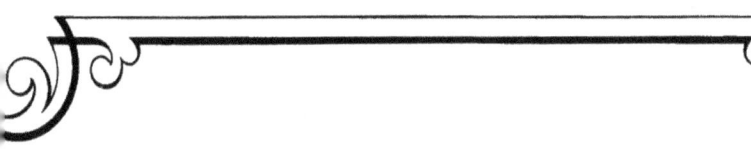

OUR CHILDREN

Sometime is hard being a parent
Raise someone with a mind of their owns
Sometimes we are right
Sometimes we can be wrong
Sometimes we have the answer
Sometimes we just don't know
But its hard to raise someone that
Has a mind of their owns
Sometimes we solve the problem
Sometimes we miss the point
But we hope that our children
Will be as good as good can be
So as we raise our children
Trying to solve the problem within
So they in turn will be all right
With no bad habits to fight in life

TO DATE

My life is normal
Not flashy or stylish
Been married twice
And hurt each time I feel my biological clock in motion
Trying to find my life to share

Dating, Oh dating has change so much
Its hard to see the pages in-between
It seems to be a lie detector scheme
So choices are far and few between

The phone and ads and computers too
Seem to mask the unseen soul
Who can say to one untold
Of things that linger with one of old

So here I am as days go by
Hope to see a friend drop by
Just to chase the cloud away
As the days go by and by

MY DEAR OLD FRIEND

My dear old friend, where have you been.
It seems as though the weather has not changed to you.
I see you with your wool cap and jacket trying to stay warm on
this very, very hot day.
Are you trying to melt away your problems for you have been
through so much.
Or has someone hurt you so that the warmth of the sun is not
felt.
Or has the coldness of your heart enfolded you until you cannot
feel any warmth at all

NOT KNOWING

Why is it that our children
think that we are Ancient?
When they see or hear things on television.
Or try something on us (as kids we also did) and think they can
get away with it.
Not knowing that things have not really changed that much.
They just do it another way.

MY LIFE WITH MY BETTER HALF

My life with my better half
Was really a delight.
The moments was always right.
The laughter never ends, and the honeymoon was every day.
Just precious thoughts of years gone by.

CHANCE

In life we all take chances
Whether they are good or bad
Some of us recover
Some of us never do
We sometimes open and close our
Eyes to things around us.
Hoping they will disappear.
But life must be on the up and up to survive.
We must talk to our God,
Every day to guide us on our way. or passed through the darkness
in sin to death.
No one said, "That life is easy, it's what you choose".

MY WAYWARD FRIEND

I was waiting on a bus one day
When this guy came walking by.
He stopped and started to talk
He talked to me by my surprise
I wasn't even fresh or sharp.
He told me about his life and jobs.
Like lovers from the start.
He walked into my life that day.
Not really knowing why?
But we would make plans just to hold hands.
And he would quickly go on his way.
But just that day he made me smile.
To forget the loneliness inside.
As time went by, we became great friends.
And would listen to each other's hopes and dreams.
He would kiss me goodbye and would go quickly on his way.
For the streets have become his home.
So, we would make plans just to hold hands.
To keep each other strong.

I LOOKED

Someone said That I was crazy one day.
And I looked and laughed at myself.
Someone said that there was no love.
And I looked and shook my head.
Someone said that fast money is good.
And I looked and shed a rear.
Someone said there is no trust anymore.
And I looked and looked, and there was none.
Someone said that marriage is the pits.
And I looked to see if I could find one.
Someone said that it is good to have two.
And I look just to have one.
Someone said, it is good to live.
And I look to see that it is no peace.

THE TIME

Do you know what time it is.
I have left my watch at home.
I know I had an appointment around, about, that time.
I was rushing really rushing to get there's right on time.
Does anyone know what time it is for I left my watch behind.

NO MORE

My heart is torn
No warning was sound
It was as though
The earth had finally stopped
The sun had no warmth to give
The flowers bloom no more
The bird's sweet sound was still
The music that was pleasant fell upon deaf ears.
This is when there's no more love to give.

THE BOX

You sit in many rooms
Black and silent waiting
Just waiting to be explored
You laugh, you cry, you die
You seem to attract all ages
You have even, enslaved some to
Sit and never move
Some even sleep by you afraid to miss
So you wait and wait until you
Are discovered in your room
Never moving just there
Waiting until someone turns you on
You show many, many things
Then you enslaved them with color, sounds and people.
Then they are control waiting for
a break to go to the bathroom.
You engross us with things, wants
Desires and dreams
For one button turn you on.

HER EYES

She wanted to see again.
The Doctor said, She's would not.
And it hit her very hard.
As her hopes and dreams had died...
But I will be her eye.
She wanted so to see again.
The new babies that have arrived.
But instead, she holds them dear,
And picture them in her mind.
She feels so lost and fragile.
As she sits and wonders why?
Her sight is gone.
She feels as though the world has stopped.
For she cannot see anymore.
But to her surprise a whole new world has formed For I will be
her eyes.

We'll spend hours and days discovering.
So that she will not be alone.
And watch her blossom into that which was locked inside.
When she lost her eyes, for I will be her eye.

A BOX OF YESTERDAY

I have a little box.
A jewel box made of glass,
To put my what not's in.
Pieces of dreams and memory
Of things from the year gone by.
So lovely it's sit.
With piece of things a pebble, a rock and a insect's shell of the
essence of time gone by. Keeping my memories alive
And when that day come When I close my eyes The box will also
die. Of pieces of dreams and memories Of things from the years
gone by.

WORKING

Working, working, working
It is nice to have a job.
Workings, working, working
Paying bills and buying cars.
Working, working, working
Waking up in time for work.
Working, working, working
The days are hot and sometimes cold.
Working, working, working
Just to have nice things to own.
Working, working, working
Is this what life is all about?

QUIETNESS

When I am alone.
In the wake of the day.
Seeing the sun rise.
As the birdies sing.
To a brand new day
The quietness of the morn
When the children are sleeping

But when they awake,
The quietness escapes
To the noise of the little ones waking
Until they are off to school
When the quietness returns

But after school as they return.
The clicks, chatter and noise.
The quietness which we once enjoy
Has suddenly disappeared

But when the children get older and go on their own ways.
The quietness will return.
But once in a while we think of the past of the noise of the
children once more.

TODAY

Today, today Just another day
So it seems that work is up and up.
With more work attached to it. What a load to do.

Today, today
Just the same as yesterday
Go to work and then go home
To start another day

Today, today
Just another day
The pay look good
And the bills are high
But I must survive

Today, today
Just another day
Just "Thanks God"
For what you have and just go on.

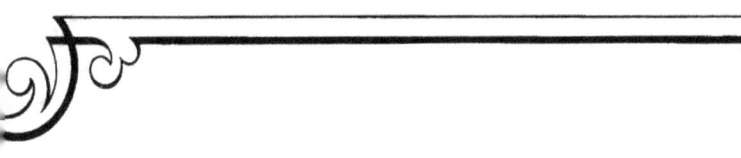

CHILDREN

Children are a blessing.
To see and watch them grow.
The time that you spend, from day into night.
Its never a dull moment spent.
Their minds are filled of wonder and sometimes of devilment.
But commonly the gifts they bring are,

TREASURED MEMORIES

THE BURIAL

Sometimes I wonder is it really true.
Have you really gotten hold of the new you.
You have shown great strength and firmness this time.
To the tee it fits you well.
My, Oh my how you haven't changed
The expression is still the same with a touch of coldness.
As we bury you today.
You will be truly MISSED.

ACCUSTOM

When you get accustom to a face.
When you get accustom to that smile.
When you get accustom to that body (Ha, Ha).
When you get accustom to their walk.
Do we just want to give up?
When you can argue and not fight.
And don't stay mad all through the night.
When you can talk and see eye to eye
When you can see him in your day-dream.
Do you really want to give that up?
Should I keep you or let you go?
It's a question that is stuck in my mind.
We just have to find out when I dream of you tonight.

EMPTY

Why do I feel so all alone.
When I'm by myself.
In a home or rooms with so much work to do.
Looking for someone to share the emptiness inside.
To fix and repair the loneliness from days and years gone by.
It is hard to find the perfect mate without some kind of flaws.
But I keep trying to find the one,
With little work or no repair at all.

WAIT

You ever wait and wait and wait,
as the minutes went by.
It seems like forever.
The days are longer.
The weeks are like years.
The loneliness seems to enclose you on every side.
As you wait and wait and wait.
To be released from the imprisonment of your home.
To be with- someone to have joy
To enjoy new ideals, dancing, peace of mind
But yet you wait and wait and wait.
Hoping one day you will find someone.
Who will release you from your home?
Just to be alive and feeling free. To have
someone to make love to you once again.
To chase away the gray clouds and let the sunshine in
But yet you wait and wait and wait.
Until one day that special one find you or you find him.
When time will no longer seem like forever,
As you embrace each other arms.
The dark day will be no more.
You have found someone to LOVE!

THE SPECIAL GLASS

I feel as though I'm a little girl.
As I walk into the large room.
The room has wall to wall crystal glasses of all shapes and sizes.
Will I be able to pick the right one for my love.
You know life is like that too.
When you can see through the glass, then the love is true.
Any cracks in the glass lose its value.
As I looked, "Yes there it is". I
have found it, I have found the right one.
With it, crystal-clear shine, of love going through.
I'm hoping he loves it too.

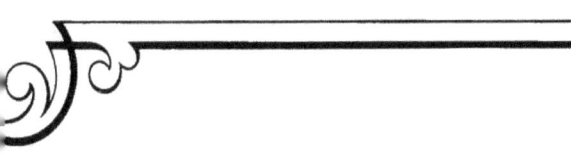

THE LONGING

Each minute is like a eon.
Just waiting to be with you
Just hold you tight and kiss your lips.
To look into your loving eyes just one more time.
To hear your sweet voice as you call my name it's like a melody in
a song.
And hoping that one day we will be together forever.
Just to think I would be yours and you would be mine.
After so many, many years have gone by.
It's like a dream come truc for me.
I'm hoping you are feeling the same way too.

M

When we met after so many years.
We had very little to say.
As we caress in our first kiss.

The longing look, of each other.
After many years of being apart.
The smile of love, once more
As we spoke our first word: HELLO

We have found each other.
By a hunger of love,
And to see that the feeling is right.
We soared to heaven delight.
Never looking back.
We have found peace.
The circle has begun again, to a new beginning.

Each one is scared to see, if this is what it is to be?

A KISS

From within a dam has busted.
Something has weakened the dam.
The emotions that were packed away
For some time has been released
The key that was hidden has been found.
A kiss upon the lips.

THE WOMANS WITH NO FACE

We had a beautiful life and home.
Until she enters our life
The woman's with no face.
And made it a living hell.
She has a touch that could enslave you.
Even the strongest man was made weak.
Our happy home became unhappy and tense.
Things would come up missing, but no one knew, but her.
No one could be trusted.
Our lives had changed.
We stopped going out.
Only he had things to do at night, because she
had him.
The days and nights grew longer, becoming two and three days
long.
She had spun her illusion just right.
Making everything looks great.
And when you have no more home.
She will say, I'll find you a home.
A house where decent people wouldn't live.
Things you would not do you do to get her.
And you would do it more and more just to please her.
But all she does is lie to you.
So that she can keep you to herself.
She bleeds you for everything you have, even your soul.
For just ten minutes of your time
To make you feel all right.
Lies with each hit you take.
We can always get more tomorrow.
Over and over and over again.
Until she has used you up.
Until you have died.
Your body is skin and bone.
Form where she has loved you to DEATH.

28

THE GIFT

It was a gift of love
From many unknown things
The colors brilliantly bright
Never dull in it light.
The years went by.
The colors always shine.
Until that maddening day when love had walked away.
The gift never shined again.

HUNGRY FOR LOVE

You look at yourself a
Long time in the mirror.
You are the most beautiful one.
At least your personality is.
But no one else sees you that way.
You try to be outgoing.
At least you think you are.
But everyone still thinks you're dumb.
They never have anything to do with you,
Until they need a favor done, they call you.
But other than that they don't call
You're hurting, you call for help,
But no one hears your call.
So, you said to yourself, I'll fix them all.
And committed suicide.
But you left a note behind:

"HUNGRY FOR LOVE"

CATCH

There is a catch.
That no one see's
They use it every day.
I'll watch your back.
If you watch my back
And get jammed on the in between.
Some of them profit
Some of them fall.
And the law is a loophole for them.
Some of us get it and some of us don't.
It just a catch that's all.

THE YEARS

Sometime the words
Seem far and few as
The years go by.
But somehow, we survive.

Our bodies changes us
Hair turns gray,
But the spark that has
Bought us together is
Stills strong.

We look at each other.
As though it is the
First time we met.

As the years go by,
Through hill and mountain, we survive
The storms of LIFE.

PARTING

Life was beautiful a long time ago
It was the life of milk and honey.
Nothing could ever go wrong
Life is at its peak.
But something went wrong.
That glow, that glow that was so warm.
Turned into a cold December day.
That mother's nature had forgotten to turn to spring.
But they try and try to make it work.
Pulling together every step.
But soon the steps seem too big.
It had come to a grinding halt.
The rope had a tear in it.
They could no longer pull the same.
The pain has been too much to bear.
So now how do you just walk away,
From a life that was so meaningful to you.
It will be hard.
Life in itself is hard.
And don't look back.

THE THRILL

What makes us do the things we
do, even when we know they are
Wrong as two left shoes, but we
do it anyway. Like bungee jumping
off a bridge, racing cars at high
speeds, HAVING AN AFFAIR, jumping
from a plane. Is it an excitement
or thrill that intrigues us to do these acts.

TWO LOVER

Keeping tabs on each other
As the days go by.
Longing just to hold each other tight.
Phone calls through the week
Just to hear each one speak.
Never saying much, but a few words spoken.
Tell how much they miss each other.
Always looking for that one day
When they can embrace.
Before another week pass them by.

BROKEN HEART

Does anyone have the cure for
a broken heart?
And why does it take so long to cure?
It's not like taking two aspirin.
Or seeing a doctor the next day.
It seems as though the pain go's.
On forever as the days go by.
Does anyone have the cure for
a broken heart?

IM THE ONLY ONE

I'm the only one left.
Who believes in knights and shining armor.
I'm the only one left.
Men and women have all changed.
I'm the only one left.
Who wants to pull together.
I'm the only one left.
Who gets hurt in being true.
I'm the only one left.
Who would trust the one there're with.
I'm the only one left.
Who still searches for Mr. Right.

JUST A DREAM

Am I not on your mind.
As the days go by.
Is it not a minute you don't think of me.
Do you not dream of me being near.
To hear me speak your name or to say, "Hello".
To ride with you at your side each day.
Knowing what is on your mind.
Without a word spoken.
Just to hold on to, to build a world for just us.
And to realize it was only a dream.

MY HEART

My heart has went out for repair.
It was broken yesterday.
The rhythm has skipped a beat.
As our love was no more.
The pain was too great.
The sorrow was too heavy.
To keep my heart from breaking.
So I will rest and wait.
Until my heart is healed.

THERE IS ONLY ONE OF ME

Am I the very last one that has survived.
Although all of our days are numbered.
There is only one of me.
The people are all different.
There is only one of me.
Men and women have all changed.
There is only one of me.
Have I missed the point in changing.
There is only one of me.
Here I am with open arms.
There is only one of me.
Did I not get the whole picture.
There is only one of me.
How the dating game have all changed.
There is only one of me.
Should I lie to just get over.
There is only one of me.
So removed and out of place.
There is only one of me.
And this is what we call living.
There is only one of me.
I'll just have to take a chance.
There is only one of me.
I'll just have to tell you later.
There is only one of me.
Another one just got away!

WAR

To war,
They fight for special things:
For freedom, justice, and truth.
Sometimes they fight for religious things:
You're right, you're right, you're wrong.
Sometimes they fight for borders line:
Move over, move over, moves now.
But we never stop to see what harm we
Are doing to keep the peace right now.

A CHILD

Do we raise our children too early?
Putting heavy independence on
Those fragile bones and minds.
Do we see what we are doing?
To the little child inside.
Does this make a child grow early?
Or become someone we despise.
So, let the child be a child to discover.
What's inside.

TO KNOW

Do we know what
Nick pick is.
Where are you going?
When will you get back?
Who will you be seeing?
And do they have a phone?
For our kids It lets us know
Where they are.
For an Adults
Have to trust
Our feelings.
Or nick-pick
Right out of SIGHT.

TIME GONE BY

The quiet time
No words spoken.
Shows many things.
Love, hurt, ages.
Years gone by
Many moons are gone.
Stop and think.
Children grow up.
Changes of time
Things done different.
But we hope
They will always be there.

PILLS

I take a pill to start my day.
I have a job you see
My doctor said, That I must rest
My Boss said, It no way
I have to work; I have to work
I'm head of the household you see I support the family

I take a pill to start my day
The bills all seem so large
I try to paid on what I need
To get by through the week

I take a pill to start my day
My Doctor said, I must rest
I have three kids that I do for
So I work a part time too.

I take a pill to start my day
I fell out at work today
My sister came and got the kids
So that I can rest a while

I take a pill to start my day
Two weeks I been off work
My bills have doubled I can't see no tomorrow
My insurance is the only thing left

I take a pill I took them all
My sister has my kids
Hush their someone at the door
Too late to let them in.

TO A PARENT

When a child breaks your heart.
Do they know what they have done?
Do we love them less or do we
Love them more and look
For understanding.
Does the child know or feel
The pain that they bring.
Does the child still love or is
It looking to find anew.

LOVE

For as long as I can remember
There has always been love.
Love has always been the strongest
Of all the emotions we have.
And we all whether we are good or
Bad show love.

Sometimes we don't even have to
Say we love, but show it just the same.
Sometimes the love for something or
Someone motivates us to push on with
Our daily routine.

So you cannot say you never
Love for that would be a lie.

REMEMBERING

I'm holding on to a good thought.
Remembering all the good times.
Remembering all the pictures we have took.
Remembering all the good food we have ate.
Then it hit me it was only a daydream.
Of the things I wish could be.

à WISH

I made a wish.
A very beautiful wish.
To share with everyone.
No matter how old or young you are.
The wish is for you too.

I made a wish.
A very wonderful wish.
To be shared around the world.
For everyone to LOVE someone.
No matter what color you are

I made a wish
A very strange wish.
To see and feel for others.
Just to know LOVE is out there.
Made me wish and wish for more.